MW00450970

PANDEMIC INSPIRED

THE TIME OF STRANGENESS HAIKU

TO KEEP SOMEONE SANE

Craig Allen Nelson

PANDEMIC INSPIRED
THE TIME OF STRANGENESS HAIKU
TO KEEP SOMEONE SANE
Copyright © 2021 by Craig Allen Nelson

Library of Congress Control Number: 2021914191
ISBN-13:   Paperback: 978-1-64749-548-0
        Hardback: 978-1-64749-549-7
        ePub: 978-1-64749-550-3

Printed in the United States of America

GoToPublish LLC
1-888-337-1724
www.gotopublish.com
info@gotopublish.com

Words are powerful
Gifts for learning and sharing
Surprising new thoughts.

Creating Haiku to accompany my photographs
emerged over the past year as my way of coping with the unease
caused by *The Time of Strangeness*.

Many thanks for the appreciation and encouragement
of my efforts by so many people.

I would like to dedicate this book to

Arlys Ousman

my elementary school librarian
who opened my eyes to the magical nuances of
words,
and continues to do so.

My greenhouse spirits
Fill the winter void of plants
With summer promise.

Surprising Spring snow
Nourishing Spring flowers to
Boost their spirits.

Look who just showed up,
Eating my green garden plants
And leaving jelly beans.

The first spring blossom
Opens us up to the life
That will soon follow.

The sun is stretching
To waken the morning shadows
As the Snow Drops burst.

Sweet Alyssum will
Spread its graciousness in time
Finding its image.

Budding promises
Known future in unknown times
Soothing confusion.

Mystery within
Gives opportunity due
Where we forget it.

The tree is smiling
At the tulips blooming first
Before the hosta.

Expanding Thistle
Stages of beautiful weeds
Or maybe not weeds

Beauty in the eye
Of the beholder depends
On so many things.

It's a temptation
To anthropomorphize plants
That make me giggle.

Fresh next to fallen;
Our lives are all entwined
In glorious pain.

Sometimes Peony
Illusions awaken an
Enigmatic soul.

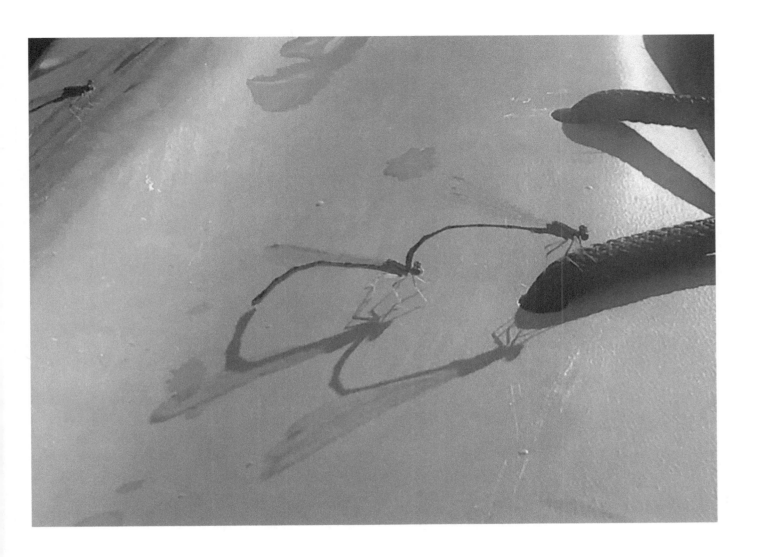

Bugs ReCreating
The green kayak's surfacing,
Reflecting shadows.

In my backyard there
Is not space for such beauty
To embrace the sky.

Swan Lake is so close
To Perfection that it needs
Nothing more from me.

A portal to where
Mysteries are held in bay
Of wondering why.

Water lilies on
Swan Lake return their beauty
With no extra charge.

Hedge Bindweed or not,
Wild Morning Glory or not,
Beautiful weed or?

The oar reflected
Mysteriously becomes
An entity quest.

Eye into nature
Becoming a fish above
Or below water.

"Mnisota" is
Sky-Tinted Water on a
Perfect Swan Lake day.

Butterfly, flutter
By, and tell me a story
Of beauty and grace.

Spotlighting Poor Farm
Bay's memories of many
An adversity.

The river tracking
Through reality into
Imaginary.

Lake Harriet Walk
In Minneapolis held
Bald Eagle surprise.

The lone apple hangs
Proudly and distinctly, all
Ready to be shared.

This time of Strangeness
Brings opportunities for
New Explorations.

Wisconsin orchard
Sunset enticing us with
Anticipation.

Magnificently
Holding forth their beautiful
Offering to us.

My alleyway drive
Ties together so many
Surprising neighbors.

Next to Rabbit Road
Are the beauties of nature
Hiding in plain sight.

Golden strands of grain
Blossom under the tower
Of powerful wind.

Reaping what we sow
Is a strong tradition here.
What do we do now?

Kasota Cedar
Another universal
Speck of Wonder.

Standing tall and straight
Promising many things in
This Time of Strangeness.

Portal to the world
Colorful imaginings
Filling my senses.

The Queen of the Bridge
Regally rules the River
Called Minnesota.

By the railroad tracks,
Another Amphibian
Hides among the rocks.

Arboretum walk;
Halloween Salamander
Stopping in the path.

I'm growing taller
In my old age, or maybe
I'm just pretending.

Mysteriously,
Prairie grasses fill a need
For contemplation.

Summer has ended
Its growth spurt, but its beauty
Continues to charm.

On top of the hill
Christ Chapel divides Prairie
Lands from The Big Woods.

Sunshine in the woods
Surprising us as we wait
For our dark winter.

Change is a welcome,
Eternally surprising
Joy in mundane lives.

A finite number
Of lines and angles creates
Each being others.

December sunsets
Make many promises in
This Time of Strangeness.

Two loving penguins
Sharing a moment in time
In Antarctica.

Nature creates in
Antarctica mysteries
Decipherable.

A Midsommar yawn
Filling an Antarctic floe
Last December's smile.

Patient Buddha waits
While the ground rumbles, ready
To explode anew.

Buddha and the Rain
Sharing generosity
In our arid world.

Buddha contemplates
As the snow falls all around;
Followed by the sun.

Reaching for nothing,
Which is something in a mind
Truly unfettered.

Thanks Minnesota
For life's inspirations that
Make it worthwhile.

I know I'm using
Anthropomorphization.
Now tell me your thoughts.

I am reaching out
To extend my friendship if
You're willing to trust.

Mystery below
The jagged edges of life
Continues the myth.

March in Like a Lamb;
Embrace the Melting Moon and
Longer days ahead.

Something is peeking
Mysteriously at me
From behind there.

A squirrel turns the
Snow golden with mystical
Magical wonder?

On a lone cobweb
An apple blossom floats,
Suspended in air.

Boulevard mushroom
On today's walk about town
Creating wonder.

The first day of Spring;
Charlie and Henry soaking
In the forbidden.

Spring's awakening
To Autumn's red remnants and
Offering new hope.

Wild Columbine
Flourishes in my garden,
Sharing endurance.

Spring time rocky road
Bursting fresh
With red and yellow.

Spring's awakening
Many possibilities
To what may become.

In '52, my
Dad let me ride the Manure
Spreader on this road.

Kasota Prairie's
Pasque Flowers I found today.
Spring has now arrived.

Many Bleeding Hearts
Tied together by growing
Vines of Caring Love.

Parallel fields
Of perfect corn rows will make
The Green Giant proud.

The lovely lighting
Makes an interesting set
To view the prairie.

Rabbit Road Twistings
Make animals of tree forms
Snaking around them.

Mother Goose guides her
Gaggle as they learn of life
Experiences.

Day after day I
Sit here contemplating life,
And sometimes I don't.